NOTE TO PARENTS

Learning to read is an important skill for all children. It is a big milestone that you can help your child reach. The American Museum of Natural History Easy Reader program is designed to support you and your child through this process. Developed by reading specialists, each book in the series includes carefully selected words and sentence structures to help children advance from beginner to intermediate to proficient readers.

Here are some tips to keep in mind as you read these books with your child:

First, preview the book together. Read the title. Then look at the cover. Ask your child, "What is happening on the cover? What do you think this book is about?"

Next, skim through the pages of the book and look at the illustrations. This will help your child use the illustrations to understand the story.

Then encourage your child to read. If he or she stumbles over words, try some of these strategies:

- use the pictures as clues
- point out words that are repeated
- sound out difficult words
- break up bigger words into smaller chunks
- use the context to lend meaning

Finally, find out if your child understands what he or she is reading. After you have finished reading, ask, "What happened in this book?"

Above all, understand that each child learns to read at a different rate. Make sure to praise your young reader and provide encouragement along the way!

Introduce Your Child to Reading
Simple words and simple sentences encourage beginning readers to sound out words.

Your Child Starts to Read
Slightly more difficult words in simple sentences help new readers build confidence.

Your Child Reads with Help
More complex words and sentences and longer text lengths help young readers reach reading proficiency.

Your Child Reads Alone
Practicing difficult words and sentences brings independent readers to the next level: reading chapter books.

For Ezra James

—M. K. C.

Photo credits

Cover/jacket: © mason01/iStockphoto.com
Pages 4–5 (left to right): cone snail © Alex Kerstitch/Visuals Unlimited/Corbis,
great white shark © Paul Banton/Dreamstime.com, tiger © enciktat/Shutterstock.com, mosquito © Natursports/Shutterstock.com,
fire ant © spxChrome/iStockphoto.com, Lonomia caterpillar © Joab Souza/Shutterstock.com, frog © OGphoto/iStockphoto.com,
Brazilian wandering spider © Dr. Morley Read/Shutterstock.com, Komodo dragon © Karen Givens/Shutterstock.com,
lion © Cheryl Ann Quigley/Shutterstock.com, viper © Matthew W. Keefe/Shutterstock.com,
brown bear © PhotoBarmaley/Shutterstock.com, army ant © Dr. Morley Read/Shutterstock.com,
box jellyfish © Daleen Loest/Shutterstock.com, python © Vasily Vishnevskiy/Shutterstock.com,
venus flytrap © Marco Uliana/Shutterstock.com, scorpion © Wolfgang Kaehler/SuperStock
6–7: © Paul Banton/Dreamstime.com; 8: © Gzstudio77/Dreamstime.com; 9: © Neal McClimon/iStockphoto.com;
10: © Jonathan Pledger/Shutterstock.com; 11: © Dean Birinyi/iStockphoto.com; 12: © Joe McDonald/Visuals Unlimited, Inc.;
13: © Jones & Shimlock/Danita Delimont/Alamy; 14: © David A. Northcott/Corbis; 15: © Charles McDougal/ardea.com;
16–17: © Alex Kerstitch/Visuals Unlimited/Corbis; 18–19: © Kelvin Aitken/VWPICS/Alamy; 19: © Johan Larson/iStockphoto.com;
20–21: © Geza Farkas/Shutterstock.com; 22–23: © Roland Seitre/naturepl.com; 24: © Dr. Morley Read/Shutterstock.com;
25: © Wolfgang Kaehler/SuperStock; 26–27: © Joab Souza/Shutterstock.com;
28: © NHPA/SuperStock; (inset) © Minden Pictures/SuperStock; 29: © Clive Varlack; (inset) © spxChrome/iStockphoto.com;
30–31: © Henrik Larsson/iStockphoto.com; 32: © Alejandro Francisco Oceguera-Figueroa

STERLING CHILDREN'S BOOKS
New York

An Imprint of Sterling Publishing
387 Park Avenue South
New York, NY 10016

ISBN 978-1-4549-0629-2 (hardcover)
ISBN 978-1-4027-7792-9 (paperback)

Distributed in Canada by Sterling Publishing
c/o Canadian Manda Group, 165 Dufferin Street
Toronto, Ontario, Canada M6K 3H6
Distributed in the United Kingdom by GMC Distribution Services
Castle Place, 166 High Street, Lewes, East Sussex, England BN7 1XU
Distributed in Australia by Capricorn Link (Australia) Pty. Ltd.
P.O. Box 704, Windsor, NSW 2756, Australia

For information about custom editions, special sales, and premium and corporate purchases,
please contact Sterling Special Sales at 800-805-5489 or specialsales@sterlingpublishing.com.

Printed in China
Lot #:
2 4 6 8 10 9 7 5 3 1
07/13

www.sterlingpublishing.com/kids

FREE ACTIVITIES & PUZZLES ONLINE AT
http://www.sterlingpublishing.com/kids/sterlingeventkits

AMERICAN MUSEUM OF NATURAL HISTORY

EASY READERS

DEADLY AND DANGEROUS

Mary Kay Carson

STERLING CHILDREN'S BOOKS

New York

Look at these deadly animals.

Can you name any of them?

Some hunt other animals for food.

Others fight just to stay alive.

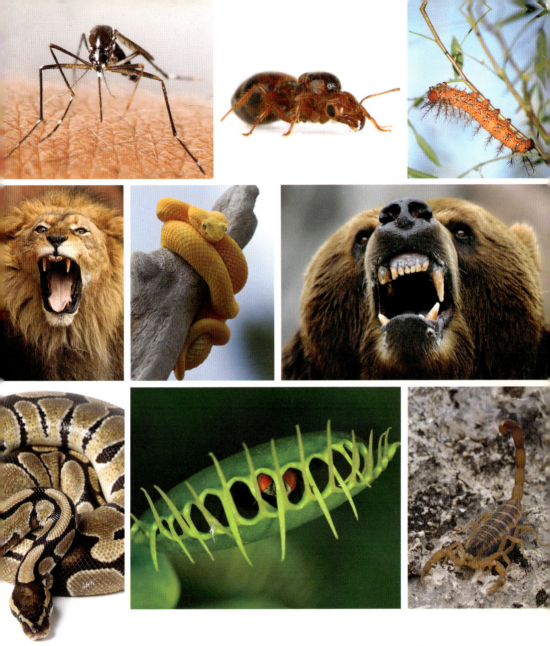

Some kill with their teeth and claws.

Others kill with stings and poison.

Let's meet some deadly and

dangerous animals.

The great white shark is a very

good hunter.

It has hundreds of sharp, pointy teeth

in its mouth.

It hunts and eats seals.

It is a fast swimmer.

Grizzly bears are strong fighters.

Mothers guard their cubs.

Fathers battle for territory.

Grizzlies fight wolves for food.

Both eat elk, bison, and deer.

Cats are mighty predators.

Big cats have sharp teeth and claws.

They run, jump, and bite!

African lions live in groups.

They hunt zebras and antelope.

Tigers live in Asia.

They usually live alone.

At night tigers hunt deer and wild pigs.

The Komodo dragon is a giant lizard.

This reptile's spit has deadly bacteria.

This Komodo dragon bit a pig.

It watched and waited for the pig to die.

Then the Komodo dragon ate the pig.

Vipers have sharp fangs full of poison.

This viper kills a mouse to eat.

A viper might bite a person

who gets too close.

This python curls around an animal.

It squeezes until the animal dies.

Then the snake will swallow

the whole animal.

Cone snails live on the sea floor.

They hunt fish with darts of poison.

A fish will stop moving when it gets hit.

Then the snail will swallow the whole fish.

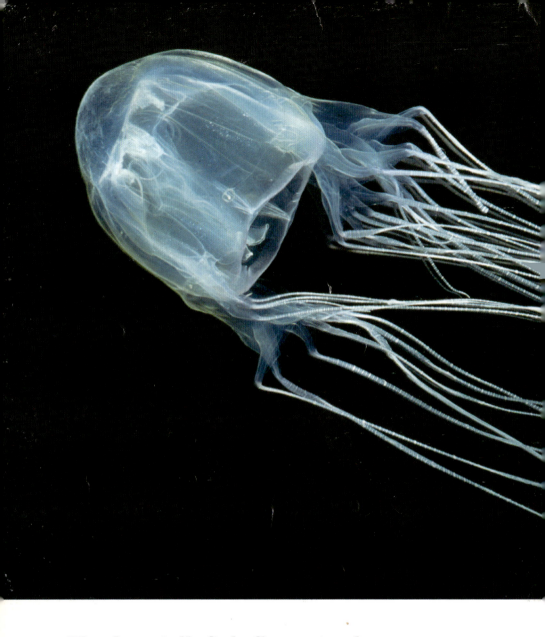

The box jellyfish floats in the sea.

Its long, thin tentacles have

deadly stingers.

It uses them to hunt for food and
keep itself safe.
The tentacles of one box jellyfish
hold enough poison to kill 60 people.

Some plants are deadly, too.

The Venus flytrap catches bugs. How?

A bug walks on its leaves.

The bug touches tiny hairs there.

Snap! The leaves close up and trap the bug.

Then the plant eats the bug.

The golden poison frog is a bright
gold color.

Its color tells predators, *You will die
if you eat me!*

Poison flows out of its sticky skin.

This poison is deadly to animals

and also to people.

This small frog lives in the rain forest.

All spiders have eight legs.

Some spiders cannot harm you.

But the Brazilian wandering spider can!

This spider's bite is poisonous.

A scorpion can sting people with its tail.

It will only do this if it is frightened.

The bark scorpion hunts for

insects to eat.

Don't touch! This *Lonomia* caterpillar
is dangerous.

Those hairs on its back are
poisonous stingers.

A person can die if stung many times
by this caterpillar. But don't worry.
You are not likely to find this creature
in your yard.

One army ant alone is not scary.

Millions of them together can be deadly!

Army ants attack as a group.

Their jaws kill bugs, frogs, and mice.

Fire ants are deadly to some animals.

Their poisonous stings are painful.

A group of fire ants can destroy

an enemy much larger than one ant.

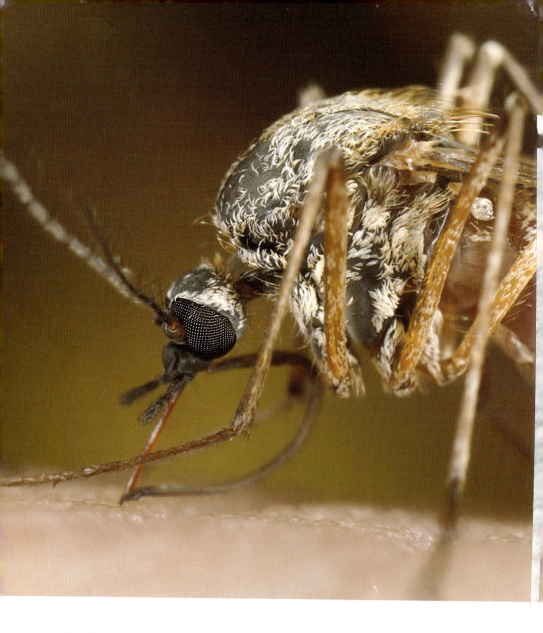

Only female mosquitoes bite people.

They drink blood when they bite.

Some mosquitoes spread sicknesses,

like malaria.

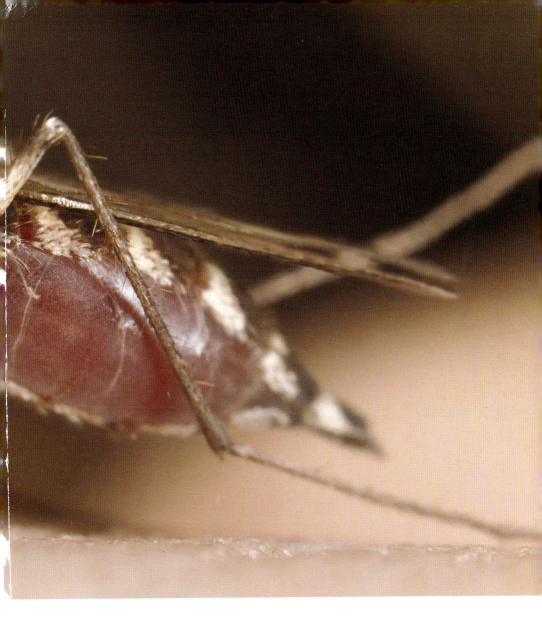

This disease kills millions of people
each year.

Creatures both large and small can be
deadly and dangerous.

MEET THE EXPERT!

Hi! I'm Mark Siddall, a curator of invertebrate zoology at the American Museum of Natural History. My focus is on the study of invertebrates, animals which—unlike you and me—don't have a backbone. Some of my favorite animals to study are leeches. These worms (often very colorful) have a long history of medical use. They are even used in surgery. I find them fascinating! In my day-to-day work, I write many scientific papers, teach aspiring scientists (including some high school students), and develop exhibitions for the public spaces in the Museum.

I've been interested in science ever since I was a young boy growing up near Toronto, Canada. I spent a lot of time hiking, camping, canoeing, and discovering nature. I'm really lucky to have a career doing things that I've loved doing my whole life!

Deadly and Dangerous shows that so many different animals have evolved behaviors both to protect themselves from predators and to find food. It's important to understand that humans have a responsibility to protect and conserve all plants and animals, whether they are big or small, cuddly or dangerous. We live in a diverse world that continues to thrive, inspire, and amaze.

AMERICAN MUSEUM
ᵒ̄ NATURAL HISTORY

EASY READERS

LEVEL ONE

Baby Dolphin's FIRST DAY · **Baby Whale's Long Swim** · **DINOSAUR PETS**

  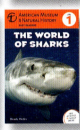

INSECTS IN ACTION! · **Wolf Pup** · **THE WORLD OF SHARKS**

LEVEL TWO

DEADLY AND DANGEROUS · **PENGUINS ARE COOL!** · **SNAKES UP CLOSE!** · **STRANGEST ANIMALS**

The **American Museum of Natural History** in New York City is one of the largest and most respected museums in the world. Since the Museum was founded in 1869, its collections have grown to include more than 32 million specimens and artifacts relating to the natural world and human cultures. The Museum showcases its collections in the exhibit halls, and, behind the scenes, more than 200 scientists carry out cutting-edge research. It is also home to the Theodore Roosevelt Memorial, New York State's official memorial to its thirty-third governor and the nation's twenty-sixth president, and a tribute to Roosevelt's enduring legacy of conservation. Approximately 5 million people from around the world visit the Museum each year. Plan a trip to the Museum, home of the world's largest collection of dinosaur fossils, or visit online at www.amnh.org.